# Christmas

# COLORING BOOK

## CELEBRATE AND COLOR YOUR WAY THROUGH THE HOLIDAYS!

chartwell
books

D1466442

# Joy to the World, the Colors Have Come!

Who doesn't love Christmas? But with all that merry making comes no small amount of stress and anxiety. And what better way to help ease the twelve days of holiday mayhem than by coloring gorgeous images of your favorite festivities?

*Christmas Coloring Book* is the one gift you get to keep for yourself. Set aside a little me-time, grab some crayons, colored pencils, or gel pens, and color away your concerns.

Why coloring? It can calm the mind just through the simple act of picking up a crayon or marker. The rhythm and tactile experience of applying color to paper helps you connect to your body. When you're focusing on coloring a Christmas scene, you can quiet your everyday thoughts—and that ever-growing Christmas to-do list.

The best part is that coloring is accessible to everyone. Even if you lack artistic experience, you can still create beautiful, finished pieces. Having guidelines eases performance anxiety—during this time of heightened anxiety—and being able to add your own colors helps make the experience more personal. And despite what your in-laws may have to say about how you decorate your tree, there is no right or wrong way to color in these pages!

The act of meditative coloring combined with the joyful subject matter inspired by the holidays are meant to work together to create a powerful, creative experience.

Happy coloring to all, and to all a good night!

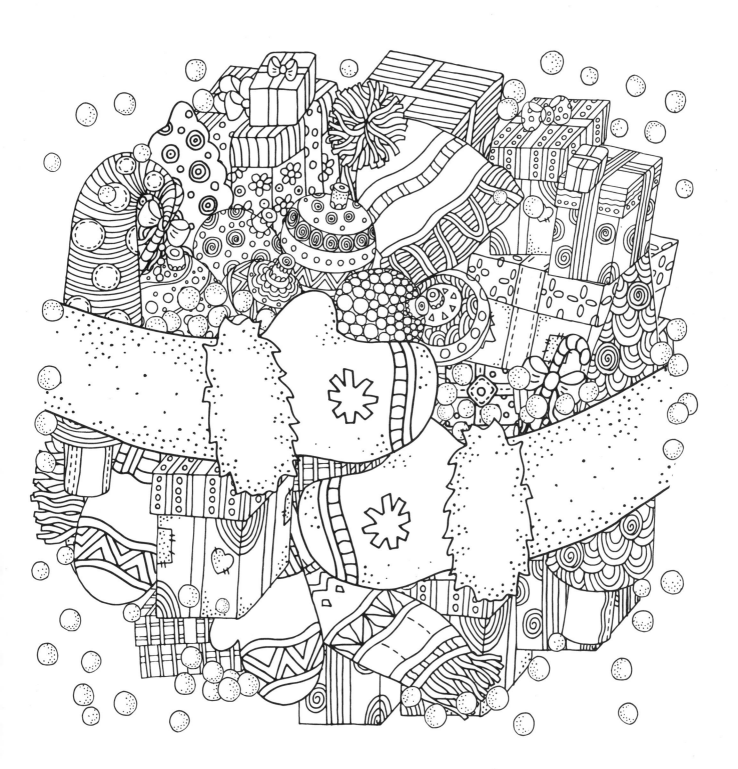

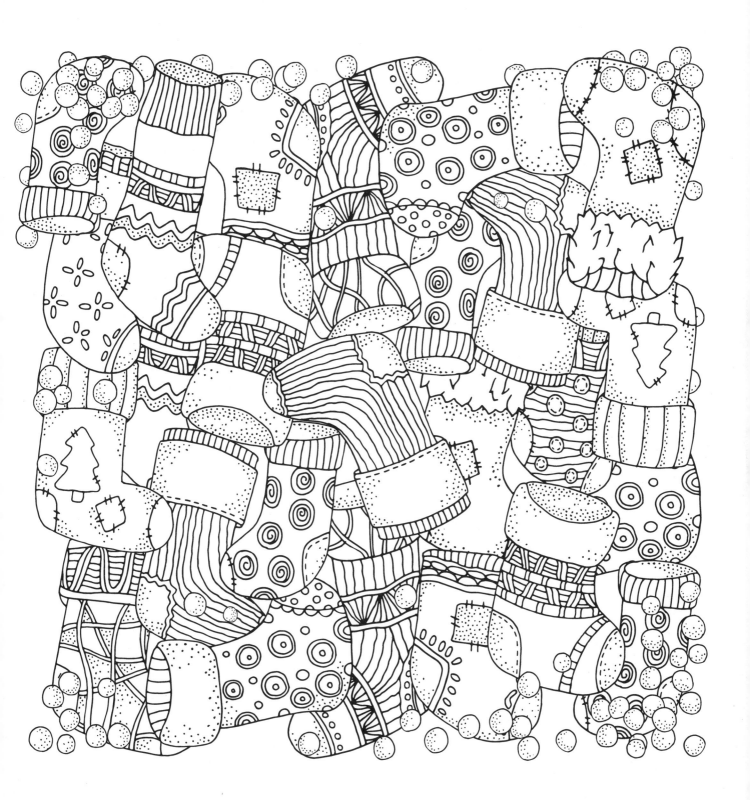

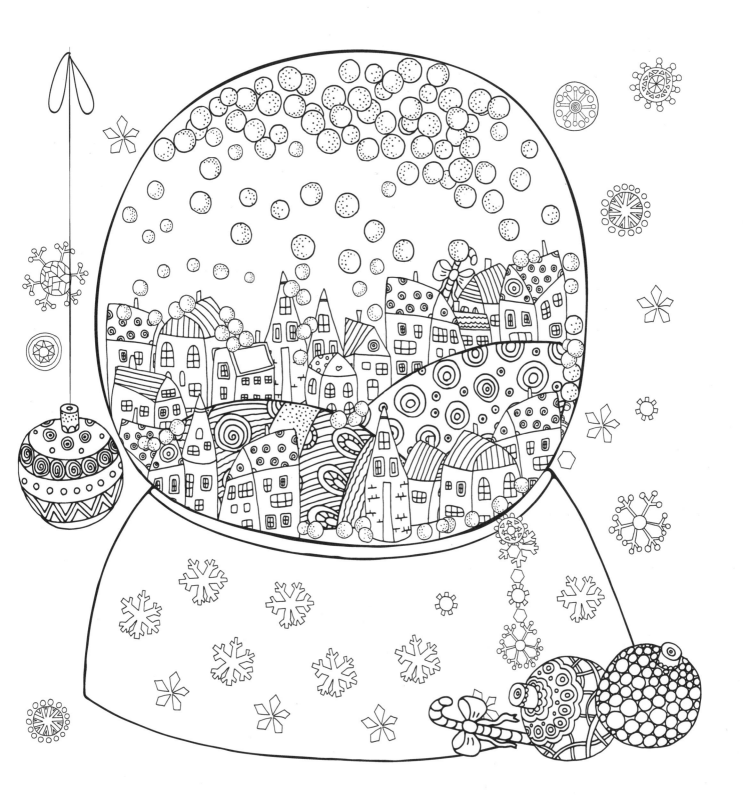

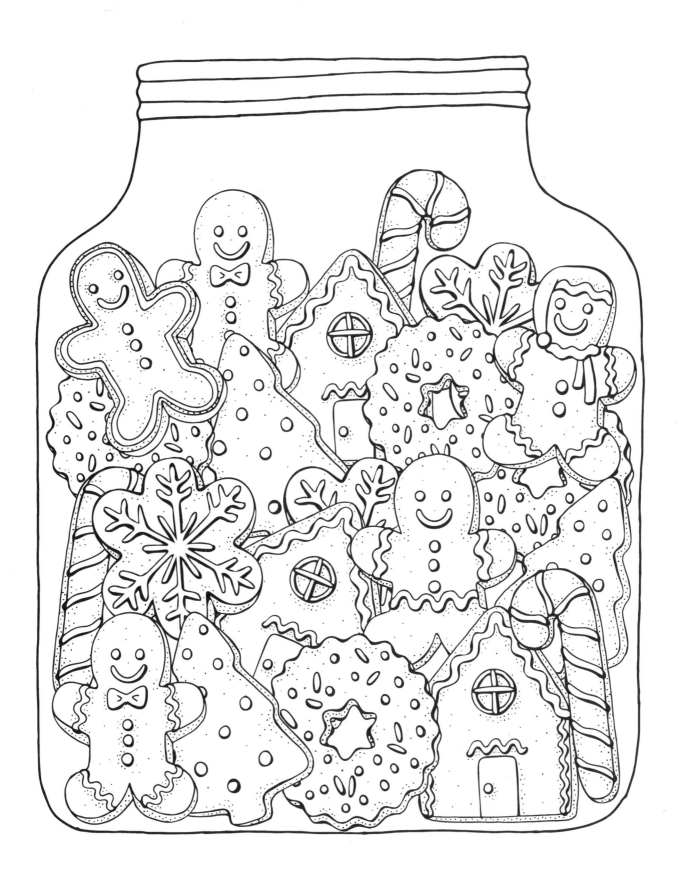

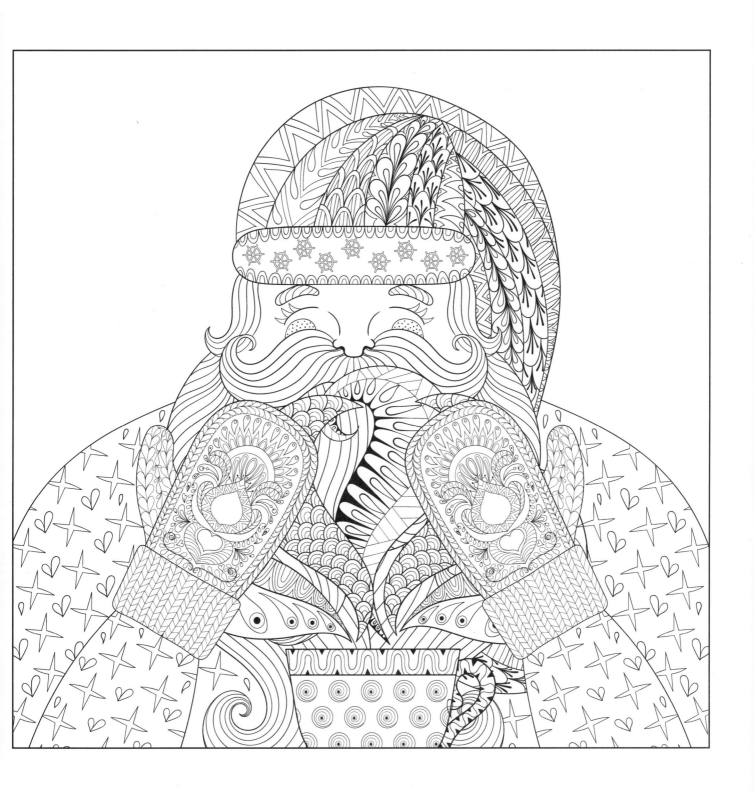

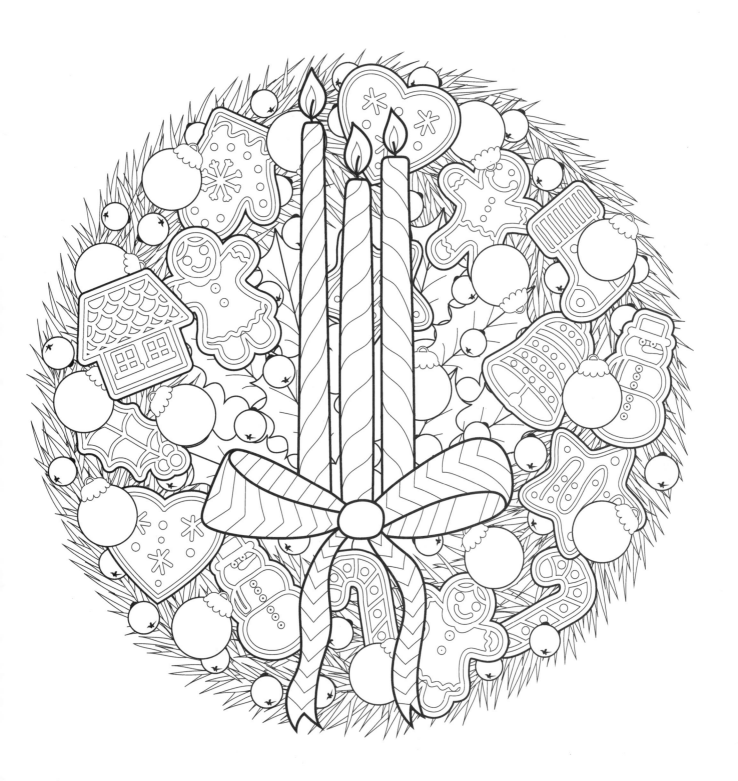

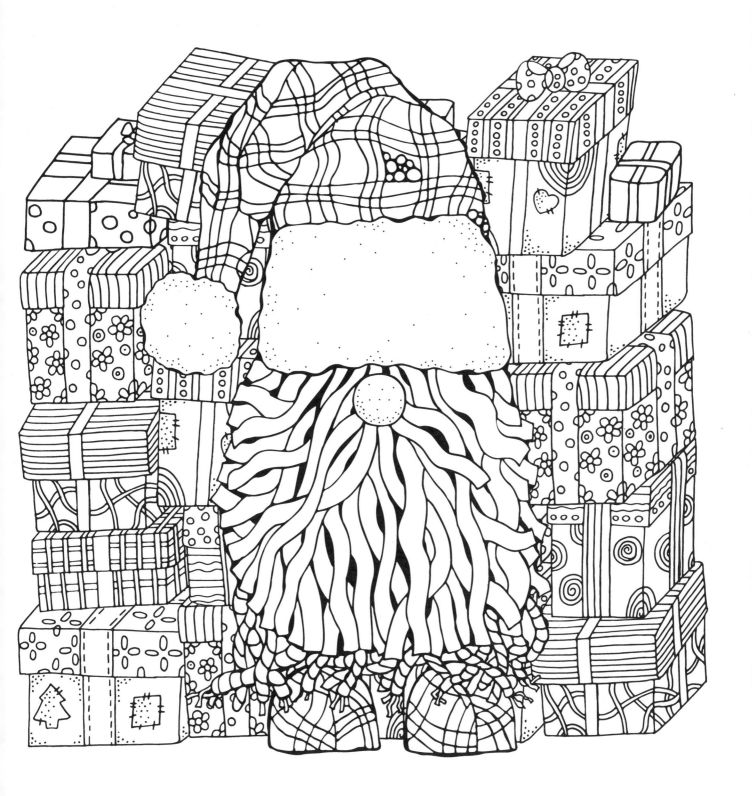

Inspiring | Educating | Creating | Entertaining

Brimming with creative inspiration, how-to projects, and useful information to enrich your everyday life, quarto.com is a favorite destination for those pursuing their interests and passions.

This edition published in 2022 by Chartwell Books,
an imprint of The Quarto Group
142 West 36th Street, 4th Floor
New York, NY 10018 USA
T (212) 779-4972 F (212) 779-6058
www.Quarto.com

10 9 8 7 6 5 4 3 2

Chartwell titles are also available at discount for retail, wholesale, promotional, and bulk purchase. For details, contact the Special Sales Manager by email at specialsales@quarto.com or by mail at The Quarto Group, Attn: Special Sales Manager, 100 Cummings Center Suite 265D, Beverly, MA 01915, USA.

ISBN: 978-0-7858-4125-8

Publisher: Wendy Friedman
Editorial Director: Betina Cochran
Senior Design Manager: Michael Caputo
Designer: Sue Boylan
Editor: Jennifer Kushnier
Image credits: Shutterstock

Printed in China